DOGGOS
doing things

T0364003

capable of knocking out listeners for several hours, auditory protection—such as earmuffs—are necessary for repotting Mandrake seedlings.

During filmmaking, makeup effects and creature designer Nick Dudman chose to produce the Mandrakes using animatronic figures instead of digital effects. The authentic results garnered high praise from cast and crew, including director Chris Columbus, who called the Mandrakes his "personal favorite creatures in the film."

WIZARDING
WORLD

RP Minis™
Hachette Book Group
1290 Avenue of the Americas, New York, NY 10104
www.runningpress.com
@Running_Press

First Edition: September 2020

Published by RP Minis, an imprint of Perseus Books, LLC, a
subsidiary of Hachette Book Group, Inc. The RP Minis name
and logo is a trademark of the Hachette Book Group.

The publisher is not responsible for websites (or their
content) that are not owned by the publisher.

Box, magnet, and book design by Amanda Richmond.
Book cover photo courtesy of @kingstoncallahan

ISBN: 978-0-7624-7209-3

Uh oH
the mailman
Should I borrk
he's usually fine
but hell probbaly
kill us all if I don't
@abbeylovesringo

beep beep
am ur Uber driver
pls hop in
we can do whatver u want lol
@churchilly

ok so basically
im very smol

the cutest marshmellow
there is

@eggnogthebulldog

this is my boll fren
there r many like it
but this 1 is mien
u can use it if youd like
u can do anything fren
@beau_thelabrador

hey sport
hi spotted boi
perfect day for
sum snoot boopin
wouldnt ya say
@dapper_domino

Whatsup quack daddy
Oh u know, jus boopin
Thank u it is much kind of u
Anythin 4 u
my golden angel
@ducksmakegreatpets

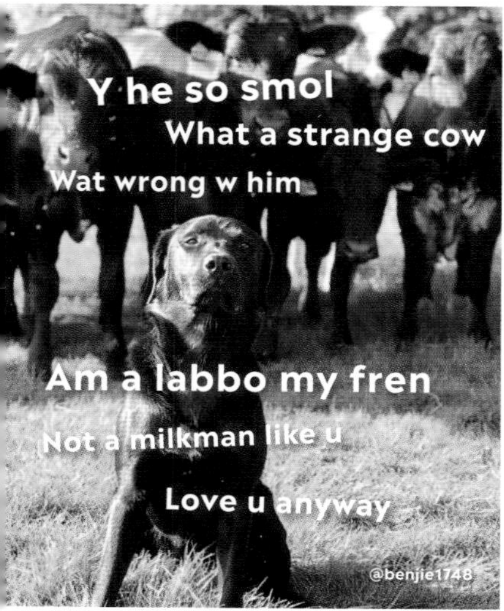
Y he so smol
What a strange cow
Wat wrong w him
Am a labbo my fren
Not a milkman like u
Love u anyway
@benjie1748

Hey there
It's me
Fluffy bro
It's ok to do a relax
Even if u can't
see anything
@fluff_bros

doin myself a smol sleepo

can wake me
up anytyme

i literaly love everything

@googlethegolden

This spotted doggo

Has a heart on him nose

Cuz he heckn loves u

@hi.wiley

if they wont giv
you a sandwich
you must become
the sandwich
thats what i was told anyway
really hope this works
@itmepepperoni

I can't be sure but

I think I know what

w.a.l.k. means nowe.

@mikeythegoldenboy

my body is so smol

i wonder why my head is so lorge

im basically just a floofy head

is it becuz i am pupper?

@filson.yosen

Vroom vroom
goin heckin faste fren
too windy to bork
luv me a water uber
i hope we lookin for fishes
@millydoingthings

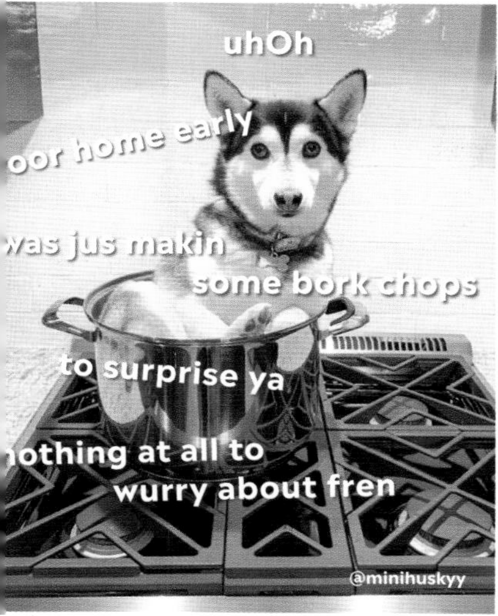
uhOh
oor home early
was jus makin
some bork chops
to surprise ya
nothing at all to
wurry about fren
@minihuskyy

Henlo humans
i brought over my
friend moohorse
can u please let us in soon
I promised her
we had snackos
@totes.the.goat

My naem is pup
im very smol
i mite be a potato
but i luv you all
@marleythecorgipup

Do u kno the beach bois fren

My favorite

woodnt it b nice
to eat some
chimkens then we

wouldnt hav to
eat tha couch

@noodle_dachsund

this here is my fren
mr gallop

he a lorge neigh doggo

always eatin the floor lol
but i lov him
more than anythign.

@valentinarossi_pup

hey hooman
just a smol potato here
remindin u to buckle up
safety first friend
careful in the vroom machine
@pugdashians

laundry day again

u know what that means

personally i hav no idea

but it seems like
a heckin lot of fun

@rambothepuppy

they always askin
whos a good boi
but never ask
hows a good boy
im doin gr8
but it would stil be nice
@redgroverredgrover

oh hey
Fancy seeing u here
think i just heard a
bag of chips open
making sure everyone is okay
@remythegoldengirl

Henlo
Who r u
u very fluffy
hopefully we can b friend
And hang out
and eat chimken
@rocco_roni

a healthy tip for ya
eat as much salad as ya want
its helthy as heck
and it grows all over the place
@scoutingfortreats

why the heck is the floor so cold today

nobody knos my fren At least its floofy lol

yep and it taste incredible lets eat as much as pawsible

@snortandsnarfle

gud morning money boi
im a cloud
and id like to make
a withdrawal
ill taKe all the chimken
nuggets u got pls
@socratesthesamoyed

Hey mom glad ur here

i wuz takin a nappo
on the floor

n woke up lyk this
heckin strange

halp

@somethingaboutbrady

hey now, ur a bork star
get adopted, get spayed
hey now, ur a bork star
eat a snacko, sleep all day
@puppynamedcharlie